LOW VOICE

Christmas Solos for All Ages

COMPILED BY JOAN FREY BOYTIM

ISBN 0-634-03289-5

HAL•LEONARD®
CORPORATION
7777 W. BLUEMOUND RD. P.O. BOX 13819 MILWAUKEE, WI 53213

Copyright © 2001 by HAL LEONARD CORPORATION
International Copyright Secured   All Rights Reserved

For all works contained herein:
Unauthorized copying, arranging, adapting, recording or public performance is an infringement of copyright.
Infringers are liable under the law.

Visit Hal Leonard Online at
www.halleonard.com

CAROL ARRANGEMENTS

8	As Lately We Watched	19th Century Austrian Carol
50	Bells Over Bethlehem	Traditional Andalucian Carol
10	Carol of the Birds	Traditional Catalonian Carol
14	Caroling, Caroling	Alfred Burt
5	The Darkness Is Falling	Austrian Carol
16	Fum, Fum, Fum	Traditional Catalonian Carol
18	Go, Tell It on the Mountain	African-American Spiritual
20	He Is Born, the Divine Christ Child	18th Century French Carol
26	Lo, How a Rose E'er Blooming	Alte Catholische Geistliche Kirchengesäng
23	Mary Had a Baby	African-American Spiritual
28	O Come Away, Ye Shepherds	18th Century French
30	O Hearken Ye	Alfred Burt
32	On Christmas Night	Sussex Carol
36	Rise Up, Shepherd, and Follow	African-American Spiritual
35	The Sleep of the Child Jesus	F. A. Geveart
38	The Snow Lay on the Ground	Traditional Irish-English Carol
44	Some Children See Him	Alfred Burt
41	The Star Carol	Alfred Burt
46	Still, Still, Still	Salzburg Melody
48	This Is Christmas	Alfred Burt

ART SONGS/TRADITIONAL SONGS

58	The Birthday of a King	William H. Neidlinger
62	Christmas Candle	Elinor Remick Warren
66	A Christmas Carol	Norman Dello Joio

53	A Christmas Cradle Song	Bernard Hamblen
70	Come to the Stable with Jesus	Geoffrey O'Hara
80	Gesù Bambino	Pietro A. Yon
86	Holy Infant's Lullaby	Norman Dello Joio
75	O Holy Night	Adolphe Adam
90	In the Bleak Midwinter	Mary E. Caldwell
95	Love Came Down at Christmas	Eric H. Thiman
98	O Savior Sweet	Johann Sebastian Bach
102	The Kings	Peter Cornelius
105	Little Noel	Emile Louis
110	Mary's Slumber Song	Bernard Hamblen
114	The Shepherds	Peter Cornelius
120	Shepherd's Cradle Song	C. D. Schubert
122	A Slumber Song of the Madonna	Michael Head
127	There's a Song in the Air	Oley Speaks
134	The Virgin at the Manger	A. Périlhou
138	The Virgin's Slumber Song	Max Reger
144	Voices of the Sky	H. Alexander Matthews
150	What Songs Were Sung?	John Jacob Niles

POPULAR SONGS

141	The Christmas Song	Mel Torme/Robert Wells
158	Do You Hear What I Hear?	Gloria Shayne
154	White Christmas	Irving Berlin

CHRISTMAS SOLOS FOR ALL AGES is a comprehensive book of 45 selections with variable degrees of difficulty. Many of the songs are suitable for beginning teenage singers as well as adults, and some pieces will also satisfy the needs of the advanced singer at Christmas time. The collection is laid out in three categories: art songs/traditional Christmas songs, carol arrangements, and popular Christmas standards.

In order to offer choices for all singers, this volume is published with identical songs in three different ranges, high, medium, and low. The high volume will suit most sopranos and high-voiced tenors. The medium volume has most of the songs not reaching above an F. This will suit the young soprano, the mezzo-soprano, and the medium-voiced tenor and high baritone. The low volume will really address the range needs of altos, baritones, and basses and could provide a useful family song book of solos for the holiday season. The accompaniments range from being very easy to some moderately difficult ones. The majority should prove to be accessible for most accompanists.

This book can be the source of seasonal selections for many types of Christmas programs such as holiday recitals, school concerts, banquets, church services, and seasonal soloist opportunities for service clubs, civic organizations, and other groups seeking holiday entertainment. For ease in constructing programs, in addition to the many religious solos, I have included secular pieces such as "White Christmas," "The Christmas Songs," and "Do You Hear What I Hear?" There are solo settings of five of the popular Alfred Burt carols and I have personally arranged new settings of eight lesser known carols such as "The Carol of the Birds," "The Darkness is Falling," "Still, Still, Still," "Mary Had a Baby," and "Rise Up Shepherd and Follow." Included are twelve solos which have been out of print for many years. In addition, the new keys provided for some of the standard solos should be extremely helpful for the studio teacher. Several advanced solos such as the Dello Joio "A Christmas Carol," the Matthews "Voices of the Sky," and the Caldwell "In the Bleak Mid-Winter," join the ever popular "O Holy Night" and "Gesù Bambino."

For the studio teacher there is enough material in this book to assign it to a student who through the years, will build a repertoire of Christmas solos to last a lifetime.

Joan Frey Boytim

The Darkness Is Falling

Austrian Carol
arranged by Joan Frey Boytim

1. The darkness is falling, the day is nigh gone, I come to adore thee, the heavenly son. I sing by thy cradle a sweet lul-la-

bye, thou art not yet sleep - ing. I hear the soft cry. Bye - bye, bye - bye, sleep sweet dear - est child.

2. Now close thy sweet eye - lids, thy cry - ing now

cease, and give me in part - ing, thy bless - ing of peace. My sleep shall be dream - less, my slum - ber the best, as tran - quil and qui - et, I take me to rest. Bye bye, bye bye, bye, bye ba - by, bye, bye.

rit.

As Lately We Watched

19th Century Austrian Carol
arranged by Joan Frey Boytim

Allegretto

As late-ly we watched o'er our fields through the night, a
A King of such beau-ty was ne'er be-fore seen, and

star there was seen of ___ such ___ glo - ri - ous
Ma - ry, his moth - er, ___ so ___ like to a

light. All through ___ the ___ night,
queen. Blest be ___ the ___ hour,

an - gels ___ did ___ sing, in car - ols so
wel - come ___ the ___ morn, for Christ, our dear

sweet of ___ the ___ birth of a king.
sa - vior, ___ on ___ earth now is born.

Carol of the Birds

Traditional Catalonian Carol
Arranged by Joan Frey Boytim

warb - ling all night long, Ex - press their glad hearts' light -
Finch his Lord now owns: "To __ Him be all thanks - giv -

ness. Birds' voi - ces rise __ in __ song, __ And
ing." Trill - ing in sweet - est __ tones, __ The

warb - ling all night long, Ex - press their glad hearts' light -
Finch his Lord now owns: "To __ Him be all thanks - giv -

ness.
ing." 2. The Night - in - gale is
4. The Par - tridge adds his

first. To bring his song of cheer, And
note: "To Bethlehem I'll fly; Where

tell us of his gladness: "Je-
in the stall he's lying. There,

sus our Lord, is born, To free us from all
near the manger blest, I'll build myself a

sin, And banish ev'ry sad -
nest, And sing my love undy -

ness!" "Je - sus, our Lord is
ing. There, near the man - ger
born, To free us from all sin, And
blest, I'll build my - self a nest, And
ban - ish ev - 'ry sad - ness."
sing of love un - dy - ing!
1
2
molto ritard.

Caroling, Caroling

Words by Wihla Hutson
Music by Alfred Burt

With a lilt (♩= 84)

mf

Car - ol - ing, car - ol - ing, now we go;
Car - ol - ing, car - ol - ing, through the town;
Car - ol - ing, car - ol - ing, near and far;
Christ - mas bells are ring - ing!

Car - ol - ing, car - ol - ing, through the snow;
Car - ol - ing, car - ol - ing, up and down;
Fol - low - ing, fol - low - ing, yon - der star;
Christ - mas bells are ring - ing!

Joy - ous voic - es
Mark ye well the
Sing we all this

TRO - © Copyright 1954 (Renewed) and 1957 (Renewed) Hollis Music, Inc., New York, NY
International Copyright Secured
All Rights Reserved Including Public Performance For Profit
Used by Permission

sweet and clear, Sing the sad of heart to cheer.
song we sing, Glad - some tid - ings now we bring.
hap - py morn, "Lo, the King of heav'n is born."

1,2
Ding, dong, ding, dong, Christ - mas bells are ring - ing.

3
Ding, dong, ding, dong,

sub. p

Ding, dong, ding, dong, Christ - mas bells are ring - ing.

mf

Fum, Fum, Fum

Traditional
Catalonian Carol

Son of God most ho-ly, Fum, Fum, Fum. Thanks to God for hol-i-days, sing Fum, Fum, Fum. Thanks to God for hol-i-days, sing Fum, Fum, Fum. Now we all our voic-es raise, and sing a song of grate-ful praise, Cel-e-brate in song and sto-ry, all the won-ders of his glo-ry, Fum, Fum, Fum.

Go Tell It on the Mountain

African-American Spiritual

Moderate Swing (♪♪ played as ♩♪)

moun - tain, That Jesus Christ is born.

When I was a seek - er, I sought both night and
He made me a watch - man up - on the cit - y

day; I asked the Lord to help me, And
wall; And if I am a Christ - ian, I

1. He showed me the way.
2. am the least of all.

D.S. al Fine

He Is Born, the Divine Christ Child

18th Century French Carol
arranged by Joan Frey Boytim

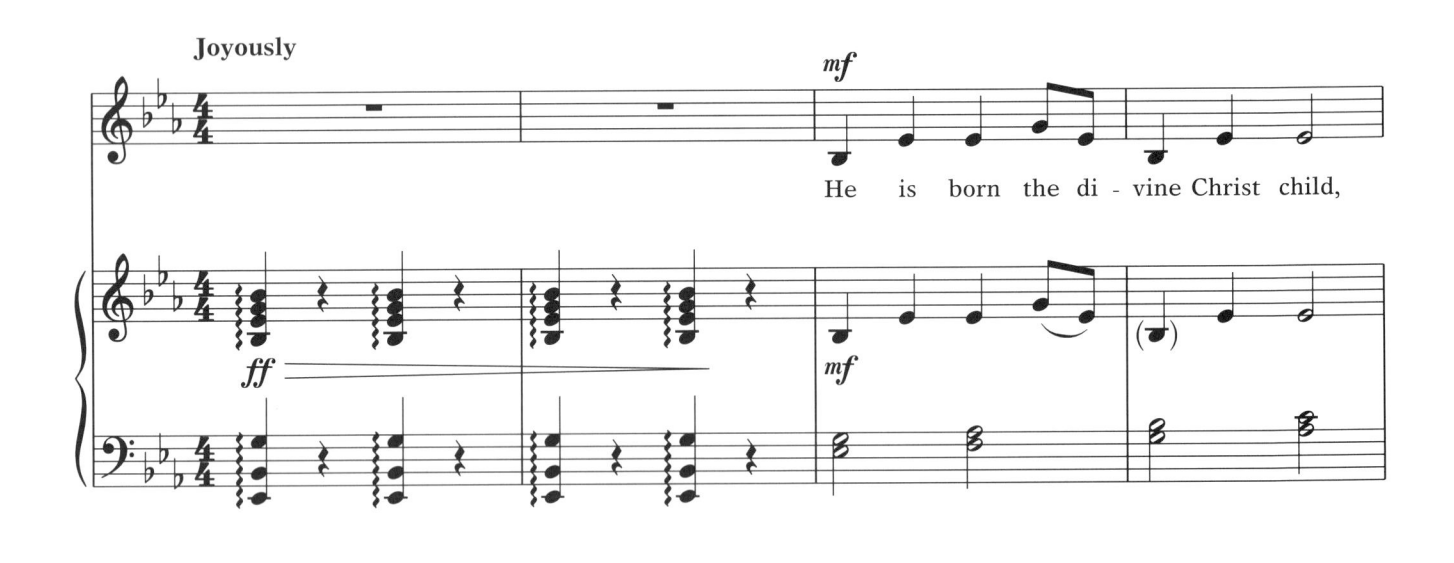

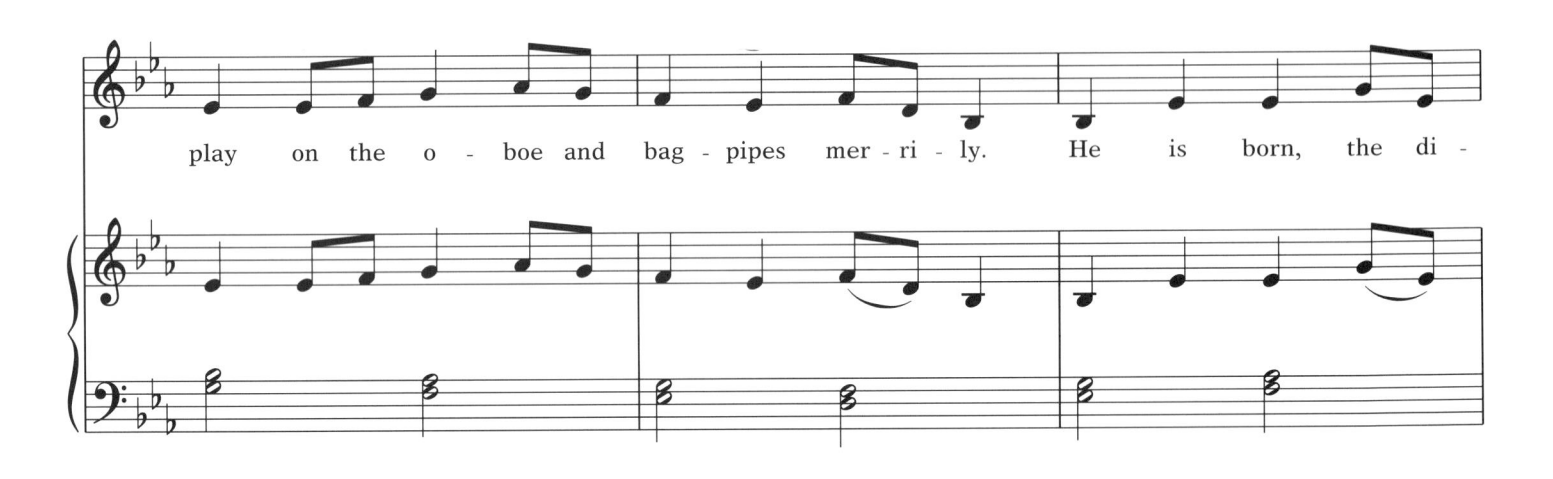

Joyously

He is born the divine Christ child, play on the oboe and bagpipes merrily. He is born, the divine Christ child, sing we all of the savior's birth.

Through long a-ges of the past, proph-ets have fore-told his com-ing through long a-ges of the past; now the time has come at last! He is born the di-vine Christ child play on the o-boe and bag-pipes mer-ri-ly,

ritard 2nd time
he is born the di - vine Christ child, sing we all of the
ritard 2nd time
Fine mf
sa - vior's birth. O how lov' - ly, o how pure,
is the per - fect child of hea - ven. O how lov' - ly
o how pure, gra - cious gift of God to all!
D.S. al fine

Mary Had a Baby

African - American Spiritual
arranged by Joan Frey Boytim

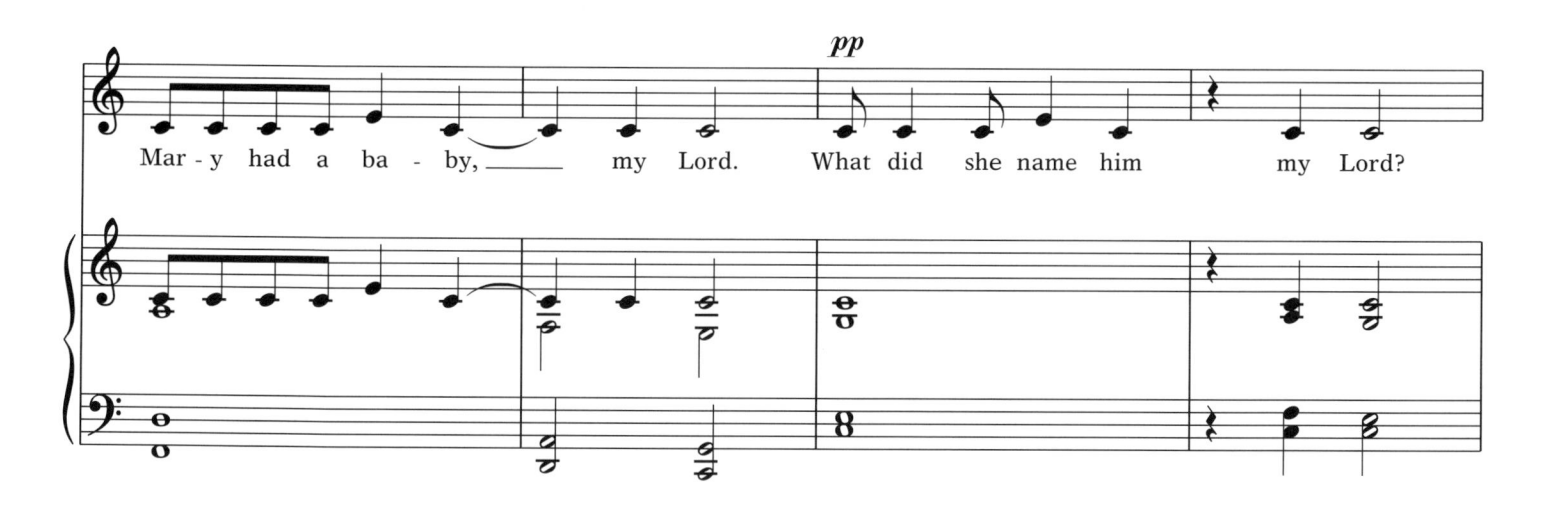

What did she name _ him, ___ my Lord? What did she name him? What did she name him?
ff
what did she name him ___ my Lord? She named him King Je - sus, my Lord, she
named him King Je - sus, my Lord. She named him King Je - sus, she named him King Je - sus, she
mp
named him King Je - sus, ___ my Lord. Where was he born ___ my Lord?

Where was he born my Lord? Where was he born?
Where was he born? Where was he born my Lord?
Born in a man - ger my Lord. Born in a man - ger my Lord.
Born in a man - ger, born in a man - ger, born in a man - ger my Lord.

Lo, How a Rose E'er Blooming

Alte Catholische Geistliche Kirchengesäng, 1599
harmonized by Michael Praetorius, 1609

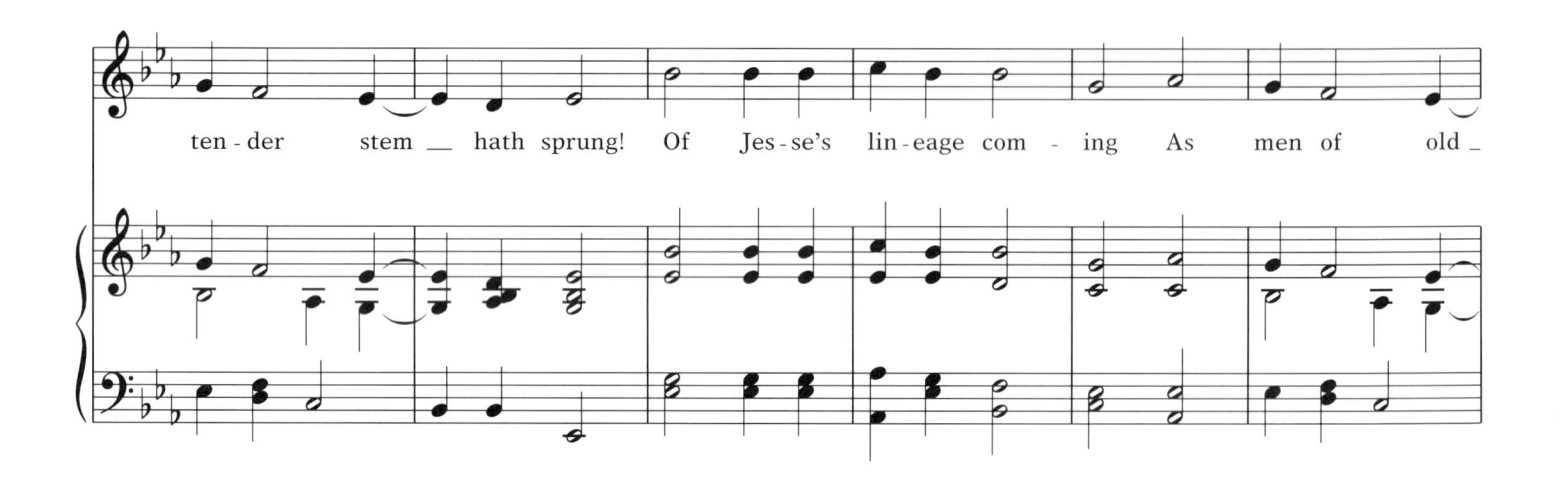

In a traditional style

Lo, How A Rose E'er Bloom-ing From ten-der stem hath sprung! Of Jes-se's lin-eage com-ing As men of old have sung. It came, a flow'r-et bright, A-mid the cold of winter, When half spent was ___ the night. I - sa - iah 'twas fore told it, The Rose I have ___ in mind, With Mar - y we be - hold it, The Vir - gin Moth - er kind. To show God's love a - right She bore to men a Sav - iour, When half spent was ___ the night.

O Come Away, Ye Shepherds

18th century French
arranged by Joan Frey Boytim

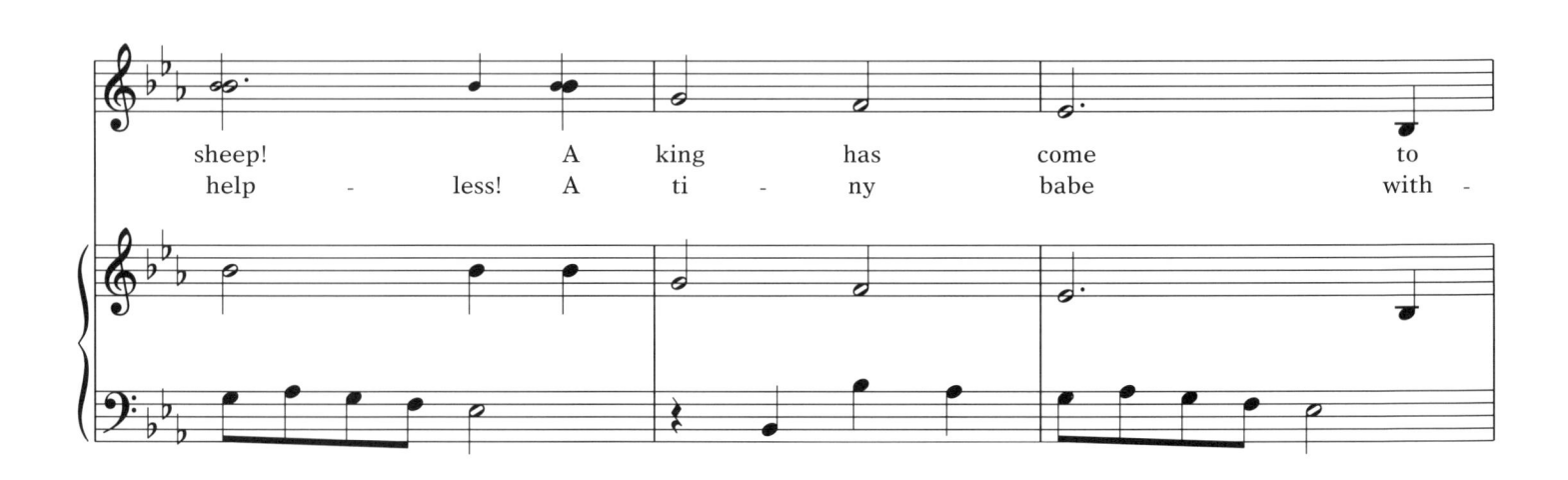

Majestically

come a - way, ye shep - herds, leave your
see him there, so tim - id, weak and

sheep! A king has come to
help - less! A ti - ny babe with -

ease our woe so deep! O change your tears to
in a man-ger laid. From heav'n a - bove he

praise and ju - bi - la - tion! We jour - ney to a - dore our
comes to earth to save us as God's in - car - nate word. He

God, our God, who brings us con - so -
is, he is, our Lord and faith - ful

1. la - tion. He
2. shep - herd. *D.S.*
3. O herd.

O Hearken Ye

Lyric by Wihla Hutson
Music by Alfred Burt

Brightly (♩ = about 120)

1. O heark-en ye who would be-lieve, The gra-cious ti-dings now re-ceive:
2. O heark-en ye who long for peace, Your trou-bled search-ing now may cease.
3. O heark-en ye who long for love, And turn your hearts to God a-bove.

Glo-ri-a, glo-ri-a In ex-cel-sis

TRO - © Copyright 1954 (Renewed), 1957 (Renewed) Hollis Music, Inc., New York, NY
International Copyright Secured
All Rights Reserved Including Public Performance For Profit
Used by Permission

De - o. The might-y Lord of heav'n and earth, To-
For at his cra - dle you shall find God's
The an - gel's song the won - der tells: Now

day is come to hu - man birth.
heal - ing grace for all man - kind. Glo - ri - a,
Love In - car - nate with us dwells!

glo - ri - a, In ex - cel - sis De - o. 2. O De - o.
3. O

On Christmas Night

Sussex carol arranged by
Ralph Vaughan Williams

Allegretto grazioso

1
2
mirth, News of our mer - ci - ful Kings birth.
sing, All for to see the new - born
2. When King.
3. All out of dark - ness
we have light, Which made the an - gels sing this night. All
out of dark - ness we have light, Which made the an - gels

sing this night:— "Glo - ry to God __ and peace __ to men, Now and for ev - er - more. __ A - men."

The Sleep of the Child Jesus

F. A. Geveart

1 'Twixt ox and ass, Thy guard-ians mild,
2 'Twixt rose and lil-y un-de-fil'd, } Sleep, sleep, sleep, Thou lit-tle Child;
3 'Twixt shep-herd youths, all un-be-guil'd,

An-gels tall and white, Ser-aphs pure and bright, Watch-ing all a-bove the might-y

Lord of love. Sleep, sleep!

Copyright © 2001 by HAL LEONARD CORPORATION
International Copyright Secured   All Rights Reserved

Rise Up, Shepherd and Follow

African-American Spiritual
arranged by Joan Frey Boytim

Swing rhythm

There's a star in the east on Christ-mas morn.
take good heed to the an-gel's word,

Rise up, shep-herd and fol-low
It will lead to the place where the
You'll for-get your flock, you'll for-

Sav-ior's born. Rise up, shep-herd and fol-low. Leave your ewes and
get your herd.

Copyright © 2001 by HAL LEONARD CORPORATION
International Copyright Secured   All Rights Reserved

leave your lambs. Rise up, shep-herd and fol-low. Leave your sheep and

leave your rams. Rise up, shep-herd and fol-low. Fol - low,

fol - low, rise up shep-herd and fol-low. Fol-low the star of

Beth - le - hem. Rise up shep-herd, and fol-low. If you fol-low.

The Snow Lay on the Ground

Traditional Irish-English Carol

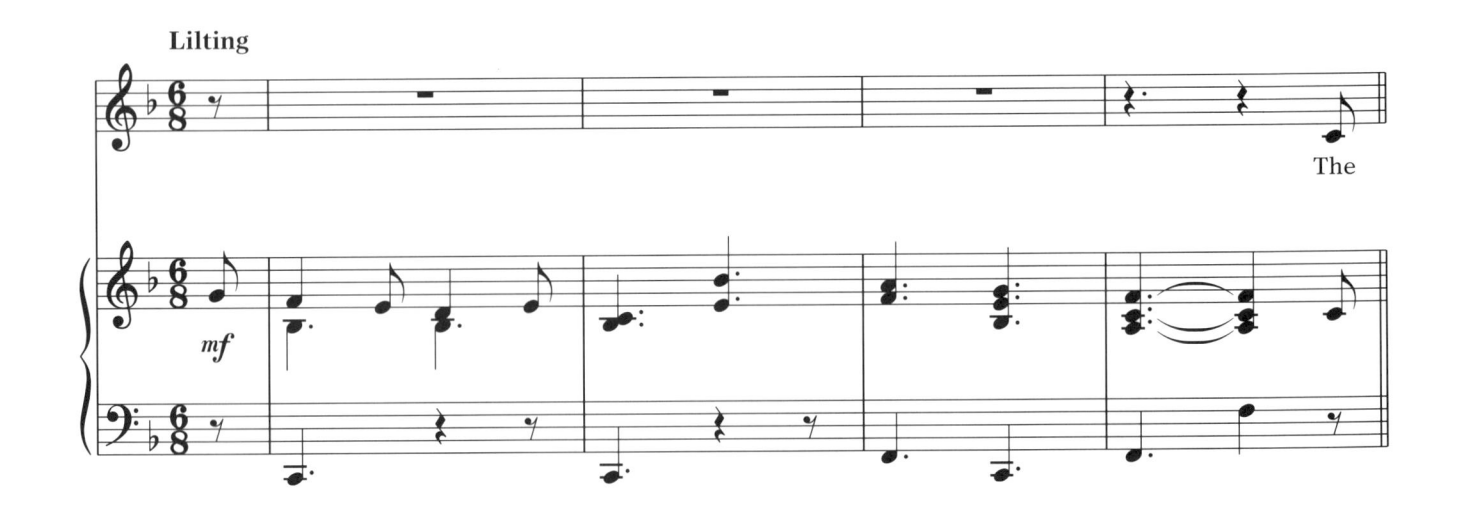

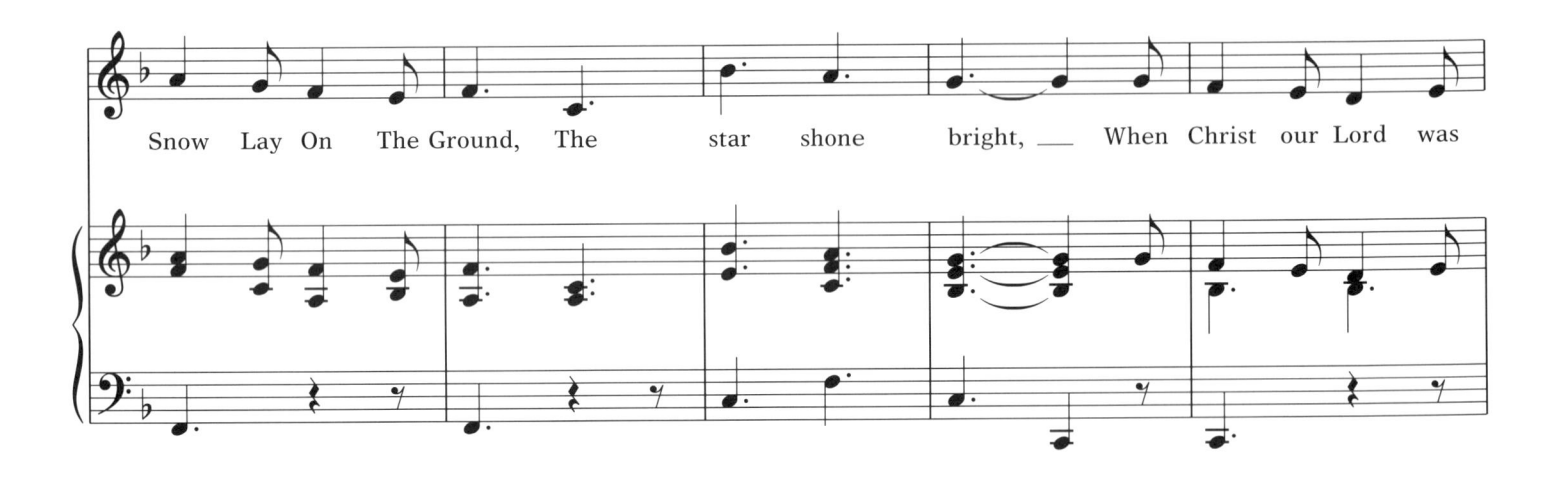

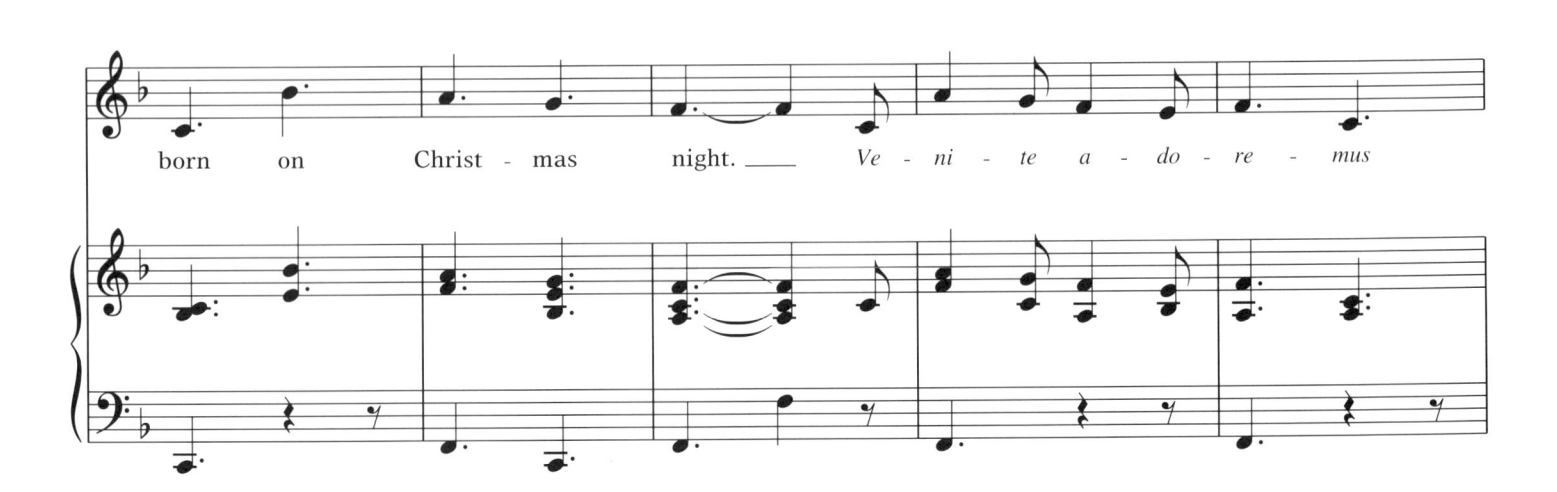

Lilting

Snow Lay On The Ground, The star shone bright, ___ When Christ our Lord was born on Christ-mas night. ___ *Ve-ni-te a-do-re-mus*

Do - mi - num; _____ Ve - ni - te a - do - re - mus Do - mi - num. _____ Ve - ni - te a - do - re - mus Do - mi - num, _____ Ve - ni - te a - do - re - mus Do - mi - num. _____ Saint Jo - seph, too, was by To tend the Child; _____ To guard Him and pro-tect His Moth-er mild; The an-gels hov-ered 'round, And sang this song: Ve-ni-te a-do-re-mus Do-mi-num. Ve-ni-te a-do-re-mus Do-mi-num, Ve-ni-te a-do-re-mus Do-mi-num.

The Star Carol

Lyric by Wihla Hutson
Music by Alfred Burt

Tenderly

Long years a-go on a deep win-ter night,
Je-sus, the Lord was that ba-by so small,

High in the heav'ns a star shone bright,
Laid down to sleep in a hum-ble stall;

While in a man-ger a wee ba-by lay,
Then came the star and it stood o-ver-head,

TRO - © Copyright 1954 (Renewed) and 1957 (Renewed) Hollis Music, Inc., New York, NY
International Copyright Secured
All Rights Reserved Including Public Performance For Profit
Used by Permission

Sweet - ly a - sleep on a bed of hay.
Shed - ding its light 'round His lit - tle bed.

Dear Baby Jesus tiny Thou art,
I'll make a place for Thee in my heart,

And when the stars in the heav - ens I see,

Ev - er and al - ways I'll think of thee.

And when the stars in the heav - ens I see,

Ev - er and al - ways I'll think of thee.

8vb

Some Children See Him

Lyric by Wihla Hutson
Music by Alfred Burt

Slowly (♩ = about 42)

1. Some children see Him lily white, The Baby Jesus born this night. Some children see Him lily white, With
   children see Him almond eyed, This Saviour whom we kneel beside, Some children see Him almond eyed, With
   children in each diff'rent place Will see the Baby Jesus' face Like theirs, but bright with heav'nly grace, And

TRO - © Copyright 1954 (Renewed) and 1957 (Renewed) Hollis Music, Inc., New York, NY
International Copyright Secured
All Rights Reserved Including Public Performance For Profit
Used by Permission

tresses soft and fair. Some children see Him bronzed and brown, The
skin of yellow hue. Some children see Him dark as they, Sweet
filled with holy light. O lay aside each earthly thing, And

Lord of heav'n to earth come down; Some children see Him bronzed and brown, With
Mary's Son to whom we pray; Some children see Him dark as they, And
with thy heart as offering, Come worship now the Infant King, 'Tis

1,2
dark and heavy hair. 2. Some
ah! they love him too! 3. The

3
love that's born tonight!

Still, Still, Still

Melody from Salzburg, c. 1819
arranged by Joan Frey Boytim

Tenderly

Still, still, still, to sleep is now his will. On Mary's breast he rests in slumber, while we pray in endless number, still, still, still to sleep is now his will.

Sleep __ sleep __ sleep while __ we thy __ vi - gil __ keep. And

an - gels __ come from heav - en __ sing - ing, songs of __ ju - bi - la - tion __ bring - ing.

Sleep __ sleep __ sleep, while __ we thy __ vi - gil __ keep.

Slower

Sleep __ sleep __ sleep, while __ we thy __ vi - gil __ keep.

This Is Christmas

(Bright, Bright the Holly Berries)

Lyric by Wihla Hutson
Music by Alfred Burt

Liltingly (♩ = about 63)

1. Bright, bright the holly berries in the wreath upon the door, Bright, bright the happy faces
2. Gay, gay the children's voices filled with laughter, filled with glee, Gay, gay the tinseled things up
3. Sing, sing ye heav'nly host to tell the blessed Saviour's birth, Sing, sing in holy joy, ye

TRO - © Copyright 1954 (Renewed) and 1957 (Renewed) Hollis Music, Inc., New York, NY
International Copyright Secured
All Rights Reserved Including Public Performance For Profit
Used by Permission

with the thoughts of joys in store. White, white the
on the dark and spic-y tree. Day, day when
dwell-ers all up-on the earth. King, King yet

snow-y mead-ow wrapped in slum-ber deep and sweet, White, white the
all man-kind may hear the an-gel's song a-gain, Day, day when
ti-ny Babe come down to us from God a-bove, King, King of

mis-tle-toe 'neath which two lov-ers meet. This is Christ-mas,
Christ was born to bless the sons of men.
ev-'ry heart which o-pens wide to love.

this is Christ-mas, This is Christ-mas time.

Bells Over Bethlehem

Traditional
Andalucian Carol

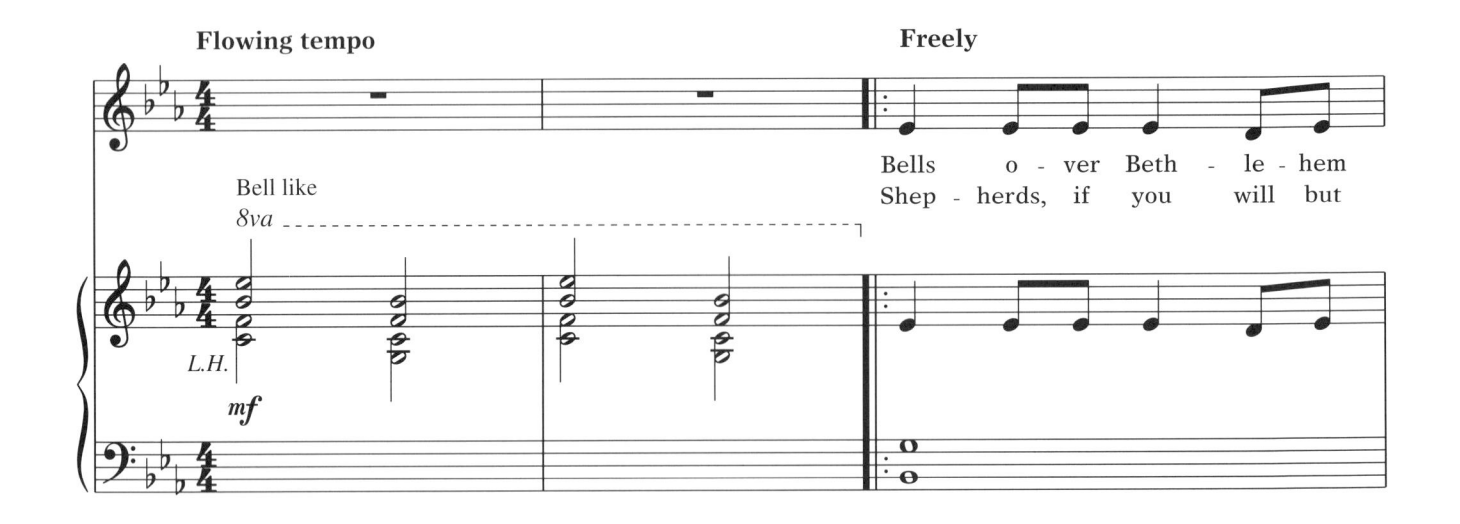

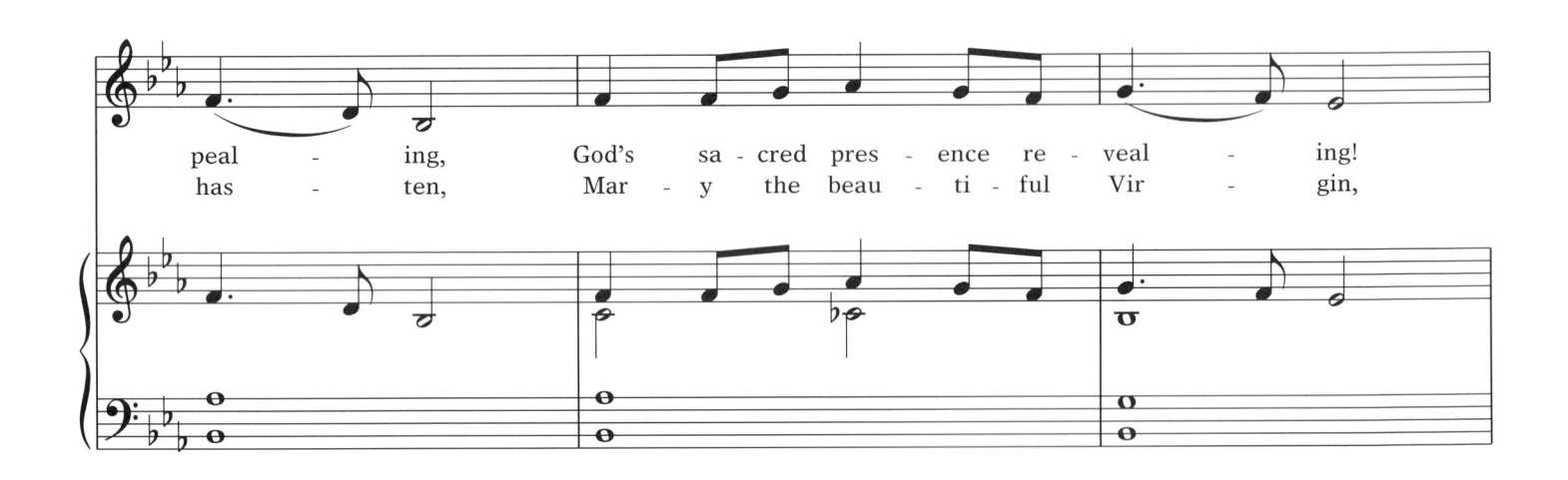

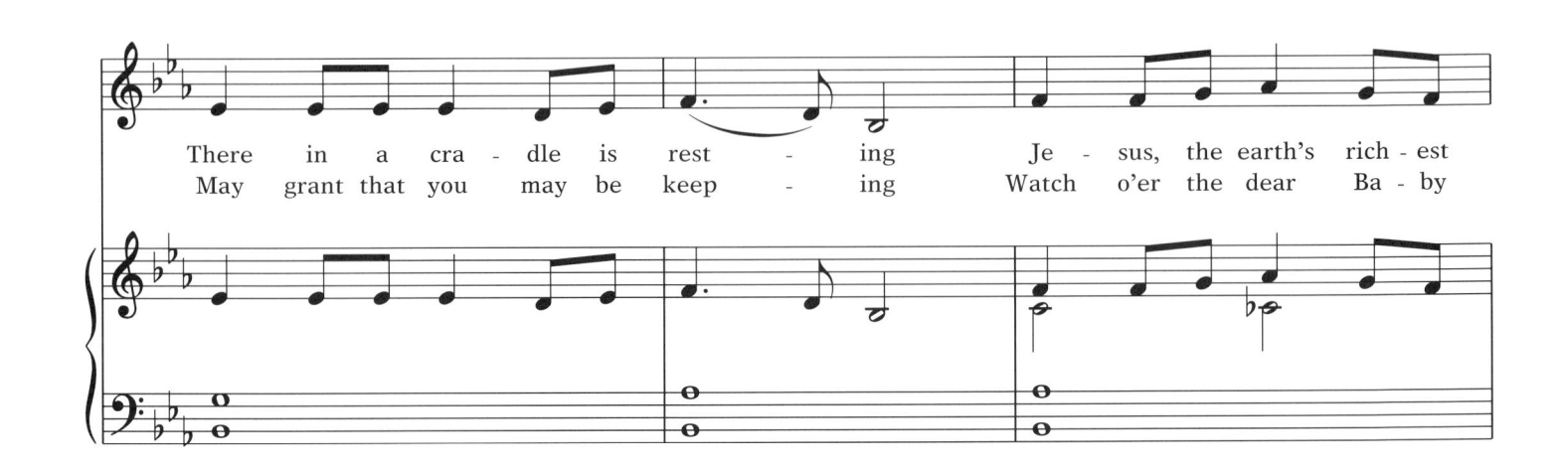

Flowing tempo   *Freely*

Bell like

Bells o-ver Beth-le-hem peal - ing, God's sa-cred pres-ence re-veal - ing!
Shep-herds, if you will but has-ten, Mar-y the beau-ti-ful Vir - gin,

There in a cra-dle is rest - ing Je-sus, the earth's rich-est
May grant that you may be keep - ing Watch o'er the dear Ba-by

Copyright © 2001 by HAL LEONARD CORPORATION
International Copyright Secured   All Rights Reserved

bless - ing!
sleep - ing.
The bells, the bells of Beth - le - hem Are ring - ing out the ti - dings, "Good - will to all men!" Leave your sheep and come, O shep - herds, pres - ents bring the Babe so low - ly.

Bring some cheese and bring some wine For the Mother Mary holy. The bells, the bells of Bethlehem Are ringing out the tidings, "Goodwill to all men!"

A Christmas Cradle Song

Words and Music by Bernard Hamblen

Moderato

Hush thee, my dar - ling, gent - ly sleep, Moth-er her lov - ing watch will keep,

Shad - ows of eve - ning soft - ly creep, Sleep, my dar - ling, sleep.

Slow and si - lent, the wear - y day Folds its gar - ments and steals a - way,

Copyright © 1929 by Chappell & Co.
Copyright Renewed
International Copyright Secured   All Rights Reserved

Dream - land voi - ces are call - ing, Sleep, my dar - ling, sleep,

Ah, _____ Ah, _____

Bells are chim - ing a - cross the snow, Prais - ing His name _ Who,

- *May be hummed with closed lips*

long ago, Came to His children here below. Sleep, my darling, sleep. Once in Bethlehem, far away, Helpless, a Babe in a manger lay, Jesu, our Lord most Holy: Sleep, my baby, sleep. Ah, _____

Ah,

Over the steppe and over the town Snow-flakes are weaving a lily-white gown: Jesu, the spotless, to earth came down: Sleep, my baby, sleep. He Who was born that

Ho - ly night Keep thee for ev - er in His sight,

rall. Pure as the snow, so deep, so white; Sleep, my dar - ling, sleep. Ah —

dim. e rall. Ah. —

The Birthday of a King

W. H. Neidlinger

In the little village of Bethlehem, There lay a child one day, And the sky was bright with a holy light, O'er the place where Jesus lay: Alleluia! O how the angels sang, Alleluia! how it rang; And the sky was bright with a holy light, 'Twas the birthday of a

King.

'Twas a hum-ble birth-place, but oh! how much God gave to us that day, From the man-ger bed, what a path has led What a per-fect ho-ly way: Al-le-lu-ia! O how the an-gels sang, Al-le-lu-ia! how it rang; And the sky was bright with a ho-ly light, 'Twas the birth-day of a King.

Christmas Candle

Words by Kate Louise Brown
Music by Elinor Remick Warren

darling Christ-Child sweet.

He is coming in the snow, As he came so long ago, When the stars set o'er the hill; When the town is dark and still, He comes, He comes to do the Father's will.

Little can - dle, spread thy ray, Make His path - way light as day; Let some door stand o - pen wide For this guest, this guest of Christ - mas - tide, Dear - er than all, than all else be -

Lyrics:

side. Lit-tle Je-sus, come to me, Let my heart thy shel-ter be; Such a home Thou wilt not scorn; So the bells on Christ-mas morn Glad, oh, glad shall ring: "Our Christ is born!"

A Christmas Carol

By Norman Dello Joio

Adagio, con tenerezza

Christ-child lay on Mary's lap, His hair was like a light. O weary, weary were the world, but here, here is all a-right. The Christ-child lay on Mar-y's breast, His hair was like a star, O stern and cun-ning are the kings, but here the true hearts are. The Christ-child lay on

Mar - y's heart, His hair was like ___ a fire,

Wea - ry, wea - ry is ___ the world, but here the world's de - sire.

The Christ - child stood at Mar - y's knee, His hair ___ was like a crown ___ And all ___ the flow - ers looked up at Him, and all _____ the stars looked down. _____

O weary, weary were _____ the world, But here the world is a-

right, _____ the world is a-right.

Come to the Stable with Jesus

Words by Daniel Twohig
Music by Geoffrey O'Hara

Moderately

With great simplicity

Come to the sta-ble with Je-sus to-night, To love Him and wor-ship Him there, With

Copyright © 1950 (Renewed) by G. Schirmer, Inc. (ASCAP), New York, NY
International Copyright Secured   All Rights Reserved
Reprinted by Permission

Jo-seph and Mar-y, the Wise Men and Kings, In mu-sic our hearts now can share.

Come to the sta-ble and gaze on the scene, The Christ Child, His beau-ty to share,

72

mp
a tempo

Come to the sta - ble with Je - sus to - night, Ah! nev - er a vi - sion more fair!

Come to the sta - ble with Je - sus to - night, Where

angels' glad songs fill the air; _____ We
lift up our voic-es to Sav-iour and King; Such
mu-sic! There's none to com-pare! _____
Come with the Wise Men who fol-lowed the Star: The

Shep-herds are kneel-ing in prayer. Come to the sta-ble with Je-sus to-night, Ah! nev-er a vi-sion more fair! And love Him and wor-ship Him there.

O Holy Night
(Cantique de Noël)

Adolphe Adam

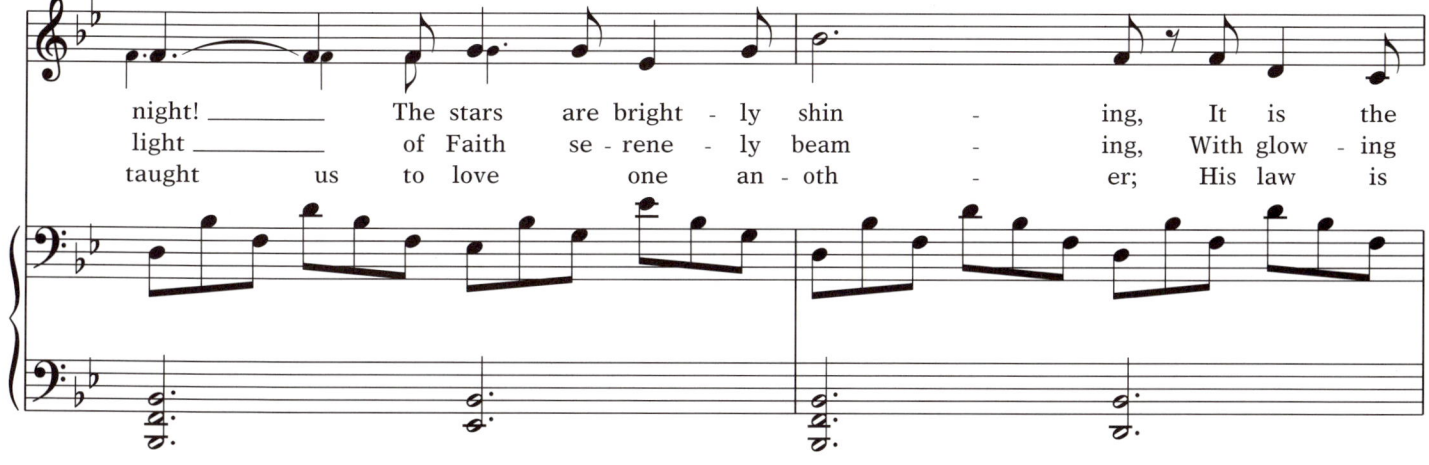

Andante maestoso

O ho- ly night! The stars are bright-ly shin- ing, It is the night of our dear Sav- iour's birth;

Led by the light of Faith se- rene- ly beam- ing, With glow- ing hearts by his cra- dle we stand;

Tru- ly He taught us to love one an- oth- er; His law is love and His gos- pel is peace.

Copyright © 2001 by HAL LEONARD CORPORATION
International Copyright Secured   All Rights Reserved

Long lay the world in sin and error pin- ing, Till he ap-pear'd, and the soul felt its worth. A thrill of hope the wea- ry world re- joic- es, For yon- der breaks a

So, led by light of a star sweet- ly gleam- ing, Here came the wise men from the O- rient land. The King of Kings lay thus in low- ly man- ger, In all our trials is

Chains shall he break, for the slave is our broth- er, And in his name all op-pres- sion shall cease. Sweet hymns of joy in grate- ful cho- rus raise we, let all with- in us

new and glo - rious morn. Fall on your
born to be our friend; He knows our
praise His ho - ly name. Christ is the

knees! Oh hear the an - gel
need. to our weak - ness no
Lord, then ev - er, ev - er

voic - es! O night di -
stran - ger; Be - hold your
praise we, His pow'r and

vine! O night when Christ was
King! be - fore the low - ly
glo - ry ev - er - more pro -

To Coda
cresc.
born, O night di -
bend! Be - hold your
claim, His
cresc.
dim.
vine! O night, O night di -
King your King! be - fore Him
dim.
vine.
bend!
2
decresc.
1
2
D.S. al Coda
tr
tr

CODA

pow'r _____ and glo - ry

ev - er - more _____ pro - claim.

Gesù Bambino

Frederick H. Martens

Pietro A. Yon

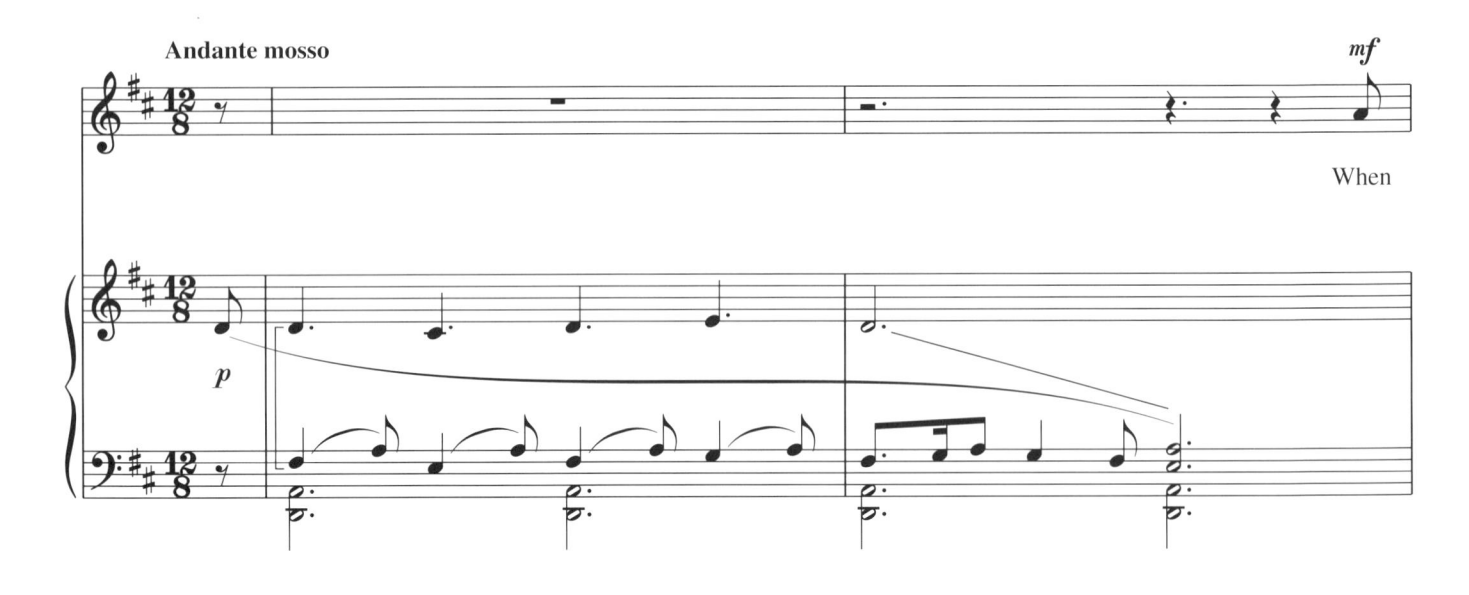

an - gels sang, the shep - herds sang, The grate - ful earth re - joiced, And at His bless - ed birth the stars Their ex - ul - ta - tion voiced.

Non troppo lento

O come let us a -
opt: Ve - ni - te a - do -

dore Him, O come let us a - dore Him, O come let us a - dore Him, Christ the Lord. A-
re - mus, Ve - ni - te a - do - re - mus, Ve - ni - te a - do - re - mus, Do - mi - num.

Tempo I

gain the heart with rap - ture glows To greet the ho - ly night That

gave the world its Christmas Rose, Its King of Love and Light. Let ev'ry voice acclaim His name, The grateful chorus swell, From paradise to earth He came That we with Him might dwell. O come let us a-
Venite adoro-

dore Him, O come let us a-dore Him, O come let us a-dore Him Christ the Lord. Ah! O come let us a-dore Him, Ah!

re - mus, Ve - ni - te a - do - re - mus, Ve - ni - te a - do - re - mus Do - mi - num. Ah! Ve - ni - te a - do - re - mus Ah!

a - dore Him Christ the Lord. O
a - do - re - mus Do - mi - num. Ve -

come, O come,
ni - te, ve - ni - te,

O come let us a - dore Him, let us a -
ve - ni - te a - do - re - mus, a - do -

dore Him, Christ the Lord.
re - mus Do - mi - num.

Holy Infant's Lullaby

By Norman Dello Joio

Sleep, sleep.
O, rest you, holy infant, Close your eyes to the star shining bright.
Sleep in the arms of your mother who sings to you through the night.

Copyright © 1962, 1968 by Edward B. Marks Music Company
Copyright Renewed
International Copyright Secured   All Rights Reserved
Used by Permission

Sleep, sleep, O, rest you, holy infant, close your eyes to the star shining bright. Sleep in the arms of your mother who sings to you through the night. A la ru,*) a la me,**) a la

* 'ru' to be pronounced 'roo'
** 'me' to be pronounced 'may'

ru, a la me, a la ru, a la me, a la ru, a la ru, a la me.

con calore *legato*

Sleep, sleep, The an-gels sing prais-es in heav-en while Ma-ry sings lul-la-by loo.

Dream of a day, gentle baby, when man learns love from you. A la ru, a la me, a la ru, a la me, a la ru, a la me, a la ru, a la ru, a la me.

rall. poco

Sleep, Holy Child, Holy Child. (Hm)

In the Bleak Midwinter

from *A Christmas Triptych*

Words by Christina Rossetti
Music by Mary E. Caldwell

snow on snow, In the bleak mid-winter, long a-go. Our God, Heav'n could not hold him Nor earth sus-tain; Heav'n and earth shall flee a-way when he comes to reign:

In the bleak mid-winter A stable-place sufficed the Lord God Almighty, Jesus Christ.

Brighter, with more movement

Angels and arch-angels may have gathered there, cherubim and seraphim thronged the air; But only his moth - er in her maid - en bliss wor - shipped the Be - lov - ed with a kiss.

hold back   *in tempo*   *slowing a little*

Broaden

mp **As at the beginning**

What can I give Him, poor as I am?

If I were a shepherd I would bring a lamb.

increase intensity

If I were a wise-man I would do my

maintain intensity

part; yet what I can I give him,

hold back   in tempo

give my heart.

gradually slower

Love Came Down at Christmas

Words by Christina Rossetti
Music by Eric H. Thiman

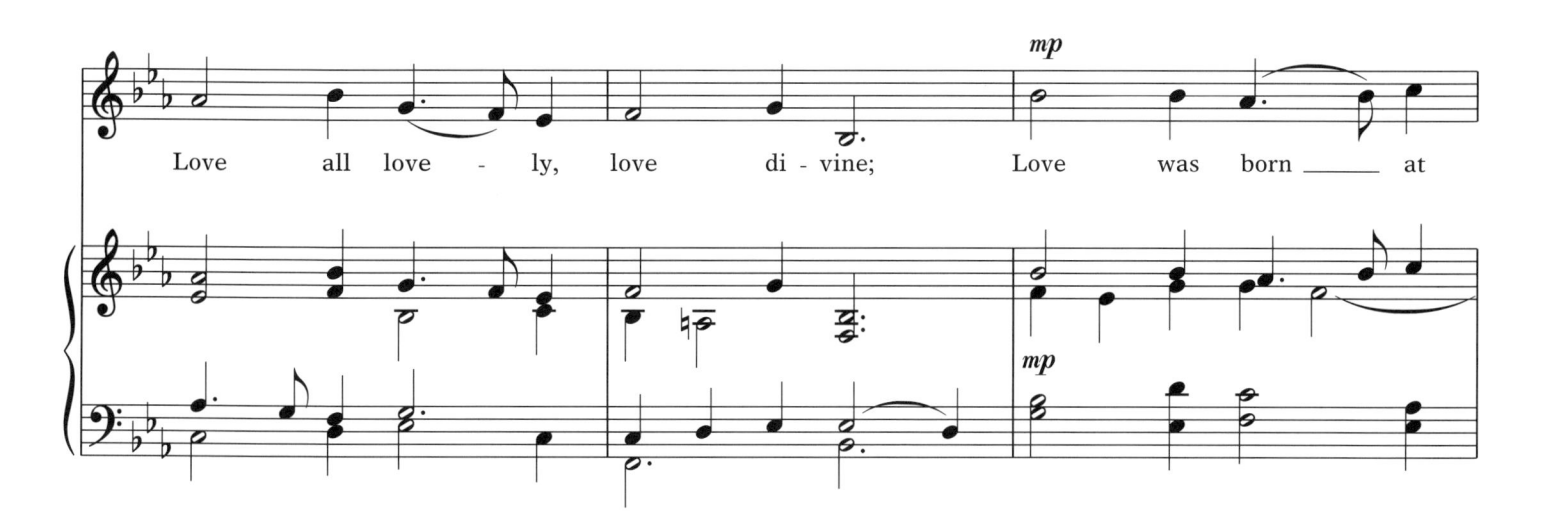

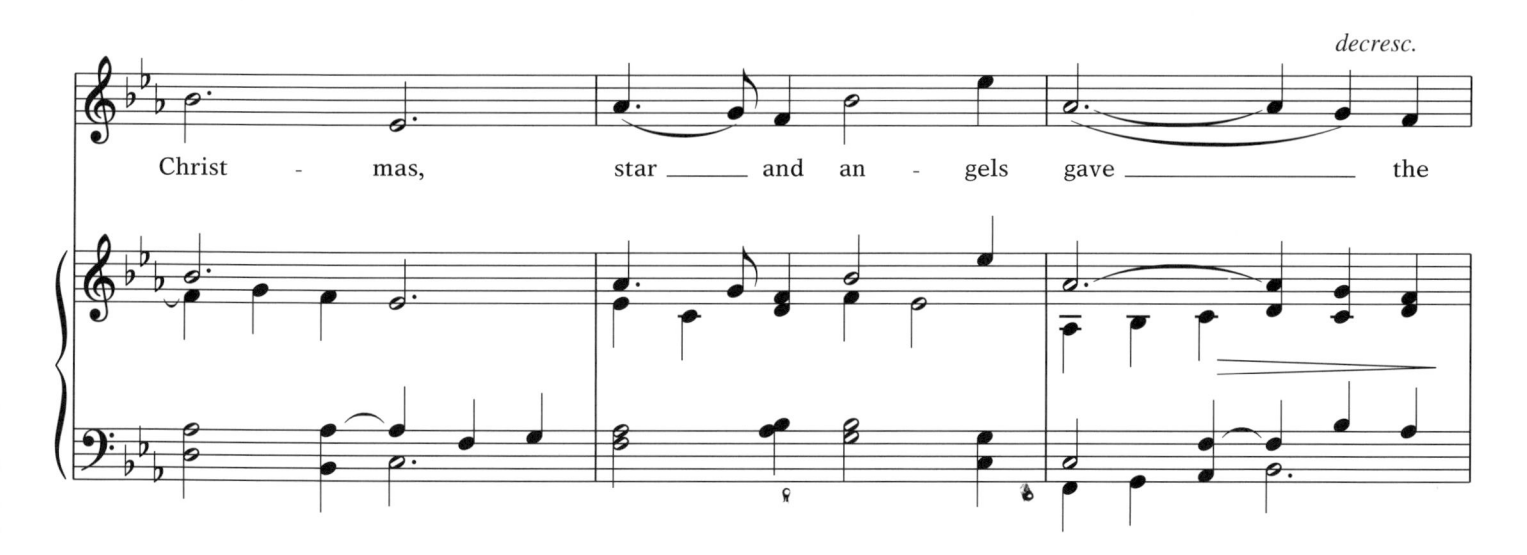

sign. Wor- ship we the God- head, Love in- car- nate, Love di- vine; Wor- ship we our Je- sus: But where- with for sa- cred sign?

cresc. poco a poco

Love shall be our token. Love be yours, and love be mine. Love to God and all men, Love for plea and gift and sign.

O Saviour Sweet

(O Jesulein Süss)

J. Troutbeck and
Helen A. Dickerson

Johann Sebastian Bach

Andante

1. O Saviour sweet, O Saviour kind, Thy Father's will has all Thy mind, From heav'n Thou hast vouch-

O Jesulein süss, O Jesulein mild, dein's Vaters Will'n hast du erfüllt, bist kommen aus dem

safed to come, With men, as Man, to
Him - mel - reich, uns ar - men Men - schen
poco rit.
make Thy home, O Sa - viour sweet, O
wor - den gleich. O Je - su - lein süss, O
poco rit.
Sa - viour kind.
Je - su - lein mild!
a tempo
p
2. O Sa - viour sweet, O Sa - viour
O Je - su - lein süss, O Je - su - lein
p

kind, The way to please Thee we would find, What -e'er we have, it comes of Thee, O let us ever near Thee be, O Saviour sweet, O Saviour kind.

mild, dein's Va - ters Zorn hast du ge - stillt, du zahlst für uns all un - sre Schuld und bringst uns in dein's Va - ters Huld, O Je - su - lein süss, O Je - su - lein mild!

3. O
O

Sa - viour sweet, O Sa - viour kind, Who came to earth the lost to find, Who died to save us on the tree, Our hearts are filled with love to Thee, O Sa - viour sweet, O Sa - viour kind.

Je - su - lein süss, O Je - su - lein mild, mit Freud' hast du die Welt er - füllt, du kommst her - ab vom Him - mels - saals zu trö - sten uns im Jam - mer - tal, O Je - su - lein süss, O Je - su - lein mild!

molto rit.

The Kings

(Die Könige)

text by the composer
revised by Henry Clough-Leighter

Peter Cornelius

Lento; ben distinto il corale

Three kings have jour-ney'd from the east-ern land, A star hath led them to Jor-dan's strand, And in Ju-de-a, in-quire the three, Where the New-born In-fant King may be? With gold and myrrh and in-cense

Drei Kön' - ge wan - dern aus Mor-gen - land; ein Stern-lein führt sie zum Jor - dan-strand. In Ju - da fra - gen und for - schen die Drei, wo der neu - ge - bo - re - ne Kö - nig sei? Sie wol - len Weih-rauch, Myr - rhen und

Copyright © 2001 by HAL LEONARD CORPORATION
International Copyright Secured   All Rights Reserved

sweet, they bring the Holy Child an of-f'ring meet. And brightly
Gold dem Kinde spenden zum Opfer sold. Und hell er-

shineth the guiding star; Unto the manger the kings repair; With rapture
glänzet des Sternes Schein; zum Stalle gehen die Kön'ge ein; das Knäblein

fill'd, on the Boy they gaze, And bow before Him in joy and praise.
schauen sie wonniglich, anbetend neigen die Kön'ge sich;

With gold and myrrh and incense sweet, They bring the Holy Boy an of-f'ring meet.
sie bringen Weihrauch, Myrrhen und Gold zum Opfer dar dem Knäblein hold.

O child of man, hold thee firm and true; The kings came hith-er;
O Men-schen-kind! hal-te treu-lich Schritt! Die Kön'-ge wan-dern,

O come thou, too! The star of mer-cy, the star of
o wan-dre mit! Der Stern der Lie-be, der Gna-de

love Shall point thee the path-way to Heav'n a-bove; And fail thee gold and in-cense
Stern er-hel-le dein Ziel, so du suchst den Herrn, und feh-len Weih-rauch, Myr-rhen und

sweet, Lay thou thy heart at the Sa-viour's feet, Bring Him thy heart!
Gold, schen-ke dein Herz dem Knäb-lein hold! schenk' ihm dein Herz!

Little Noel
(Petit Noël)

Theophile Gautier
English version by
Margaret Aliona Dole

Emile Louis

Allegretto

The night is dark, with snow descending,
Bells, gayly chime a festal song!
The Christ is born! The Christ is born!

*Le ciel est noir, la terre est blanche;
Cloches, carillonnez gaîment!
Jésus est né, Jésus est né;*

Copyright © 2001 by HAL LEONARD CORPORATION
International Copyright Secured   All Rights Reserved

His Moth-er bend-ing o'er him
La Vier-ge pen-che sur lui

smiles up-on his face sub-lime.
son vi-sa-ge char-mant.

Bells, gay-ly chime a fes-tal song! The
Clo-ches, ca-ril-lon-nez gaî-ment! Jé-

Christ is born! The Christ is born!
sus est né, Jé-sus est né.

No warm, white cov-'ring in the man - ger
Pas de cour - ti - nes fes - ton - né - es

To keep the Babe from bit - ter cold; On - ly the
Pour pré - ser - ver l'en - fant du froid; Rien que des

cob - webs for the stran - ger From raf - ters high they
toi - les d'a - rai - gné - es Qui pen - dent des

hang gray and old.
pou - tres du toit.

a tempo
p

He on the fra-grant hay is sleep - ing, warmed by the breath of
Il trem - ble sur la pa - ille fraî - che, Ce cher pe - tit en -

friend - ly cow; The ox - en gen - tle watch are
fant Jé - sus, Et pour l'é - chauf - fer dans sa

keep - ing A - round the lit - tle Child di -
crè - che L'âne et le bœuf souf - flent des -

poco rit. **Un peu plus lent**
p

vine. The snow up -
sus. La neige au

pp

on the roof piles high - er, But Heav-en o-pened where it
chau - me coud ses fran - ges, Mais sur le toit s'ou - vre le

fell. Hark! All in white the an-gel-
ciel Et, tout en blanc, le chœur des

choir To shep-herds sing, No-ël! No-
an - ges Chante aux ber - gers: No-ël! No-

ël!
ël!

Mary's Slumber Song

Words and Music by Bernard Hamblen

Andante grazioso

Sleep, little Lord Jesus, Angels hover near; In Thy lowly cradle Sleep, and do not fear: Peaceful be Thy

Copyright © 1937 by Chappell & Co.
Copyright Renewed
International Copyright Secured   All Rights Reserved

*A lightly open "Ah" may be substituted for humming.

Mm _____ Mm _____

poco rit.

a tempo ... *rit.*

Mm _____ Mm _____

p *a tempo*

Hush, lit - tle Lord Je - sus, Soon will come _ the day, Sha - dows round _ Thy cra - dle

Gent - ly steal a - way:
mp
May the Fa - ther
mp
keep Thee
Ev - er in His sight,
p
rit.
p
rit.
ten.
ten.
ten.
Sleep, lit - tle Lord Je - sus,
Till the morn - ing light.
p
rit.
pp
Mm
pp
rit.
pp
ppp

The Shepherds
(Die Hirten)

Peter Cornelius
Translation by Henry Clough-Leightner

Peter Cornelius

Andante: tranquillamente

Shep-herds are watch-ing their sheep;
Hir - ten wa - chen im Feld;

Earth is hush'd in sleep;
Nacht ist rings auf der Welt;

They in the mead-ows a - lone are wa - king, The
wach sind die Hir - ten al - lei - ne im Hai - ne, die

Copyright © 2001 by HAL LEONARD CORPORATION
International Copyright Secured   All Rights Reserved

shep - herds a - lone _ are wa - king.
Hir - ten al - lei - ne im Hai - ne.

And an an - gel of light
Und ein En - gel so licht

Tell - eth the shep - herds this night: "Christ, Re - deem - er of na - tions,
grü - sset die Hir - ten und spricht: "Christ, das Heil al - ler From - men, ist

com - eth, Re - deem - er of na - tions, He
kom - men! das Heil al - ler From - men ist

com - eth!"
kom - men!"

(poco rit.)

a tempo *mf*
An - gels sing with ac - cord; "Glo -
En - gel sin - gen um - her: "Gott

cresc.
poco
- ry be to the Lord! And on earth peace and
im Him - mel sei Ehr'! Und den Men - schen hie -
cresc.
poco
largamente
mf a tempo
good - will to mor - tals! On
nie - den sei Frie - den! Den
largamente
dim.
a tempo
earth be good - will
Men schen hie - nie - den
mp
mf

(Sheet music, page 118)

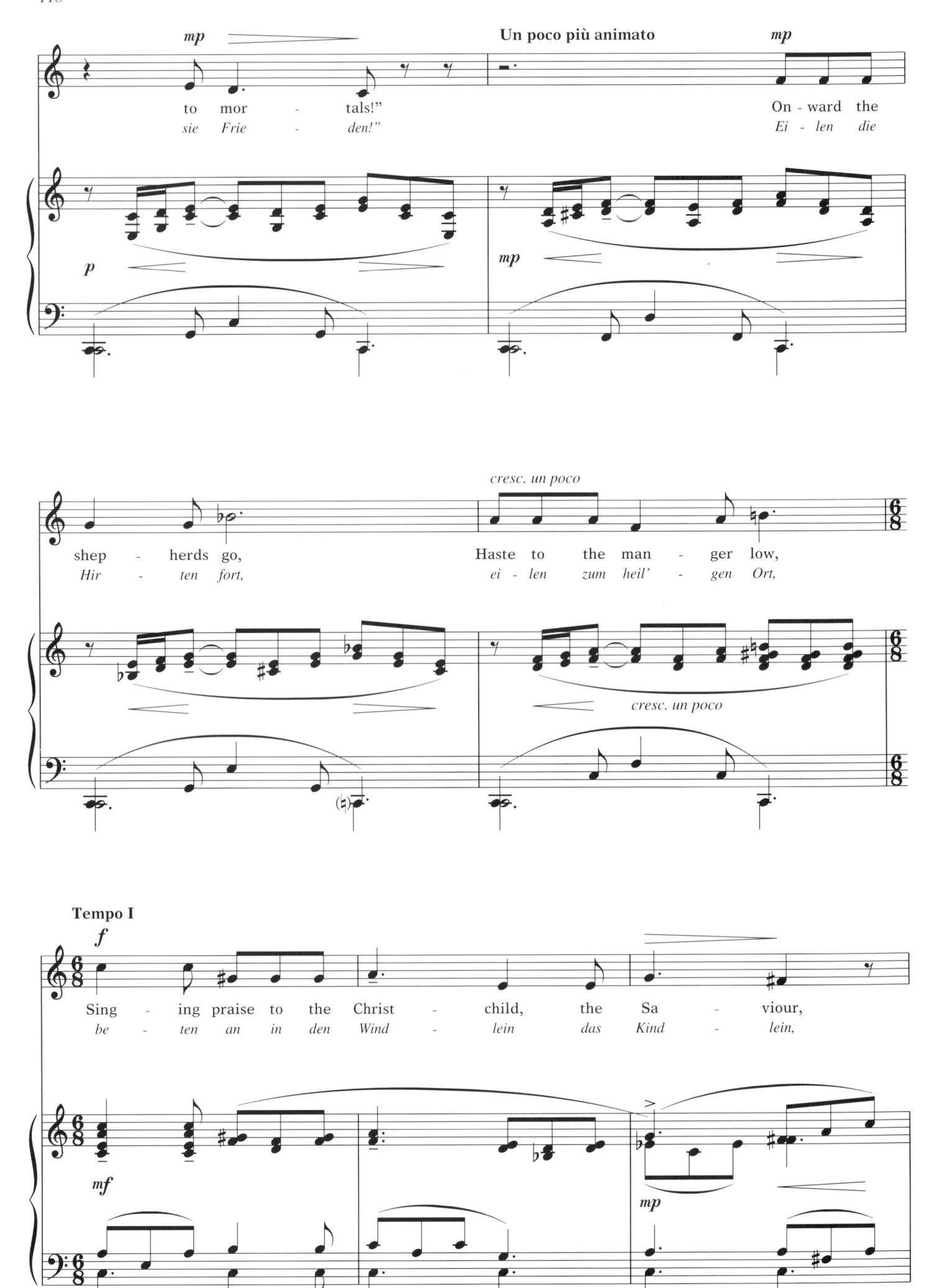

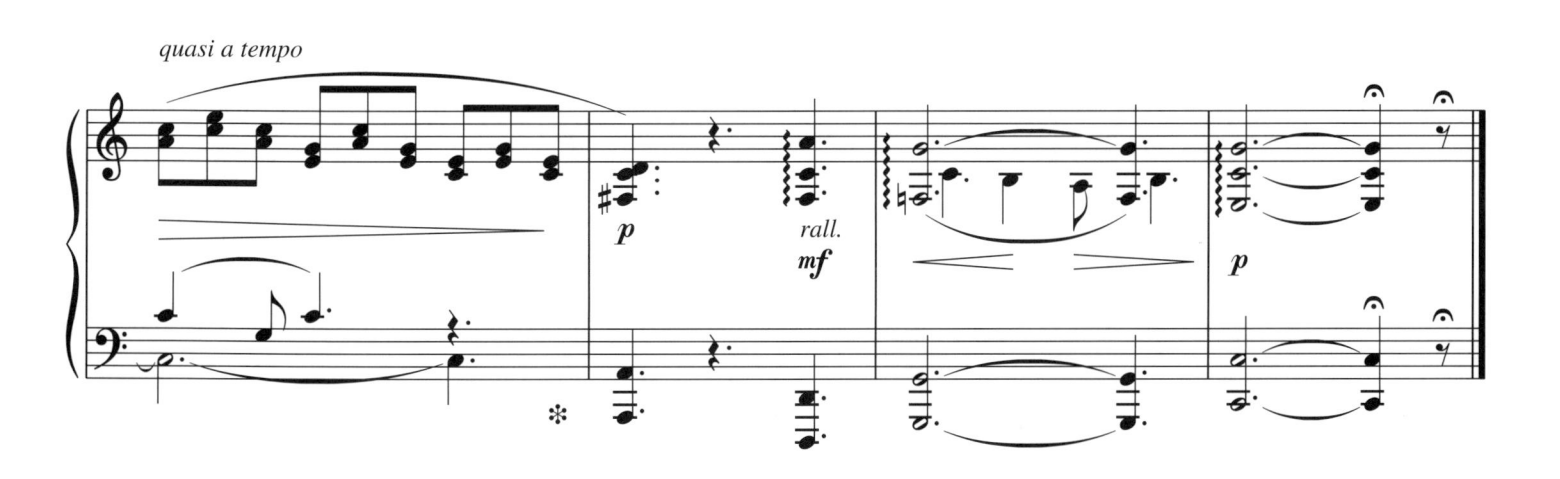

Sing - ing praise _____ to the Christ - child, the Sa - viour.
be - ten an _____ in den Wind - lein das Kind - lein.

Shepherd's Cradle Song

Words and Music by
C.D. Schubert

Flowing

Sleep well, Thou love- ly heav'n- ly Babe. Sleep well, Thou sweet- est Child, _____ While an- gels with ____ their soft white

Sleep well while Ma- ry holds Thee close. Sleep well up- on ____ her breast, _____ Dear Jo- seph scarce- ly dares to

Copyright © 2001 by HAL LEONARD CORPORATION
International Copyright Secured   All Rights Reserved

wings Stir breez - es, cool and mild. We
breathe; He'd not dis - turb Thy rest! The

shep - herds poor will sing to Thee A lull - a -
lambs stand mute a - bout the stall As they a -

by, so ten - der - ly:
dore Thee, Lord of all!
Sleep, sleep

Sleep, sleep Lit - tle Son of Heav - en, sleep!

A Slumber Song of the Madonna

Alfred Noyes

Michael Head

Andante espressivo

Sleep, _____ lit-tle ba-by, I love thee;

Copyright © 2001 by HAL LEONARD CORPORATION
International Copyright Secured   All Rights Reserved

Sleep, little king I am bending above thee!

How should I know what to sing

Here in my arms as I swing thee to sleep?

Hush - a - by low, Rock - a - by so,

Kings may have won - der - ful jew - els to bring,

Mother has only a kiss for her king!

Why should my singing so make me to weep? On-

-ly I know that I love thee, I love thee,

Love thee, my little one, sleep, sleep, sleep, sleep, sleep.

There's a Song in the Air

J.G. Holland

Oley Speaks

Andante con moto

mp

p lento tranquillo

Peace on the earth,

rit.

pp lento tranquillo

Good-will to men, peace on the earth.

poco cresc.

rit.

Andantino semplice

pp

Copyright © 2001 by HAL LEONARD CORPORATION
International Copyright Secured   All Rights Reserved

Allegretto con moto

There's a song in the air, There's a star in the sky, There's a mother's deep pray'r, And a baby's low cry; And the star rains its fire While the Beautiful sing, For the manger of

rit.

Beth - le - hem cra - dles a King. There's a

più animato

tu - mult of joy O'er the won - der - ful

cresc.

birth, For the Vir - gin's sweet boy Is the

Lord of the earth. And the star rains its fire While the

Beau-ti-ful sing, For the man-ger of Beth-le-hem cra-dles a King.

Maestoso ($\mathrel{\unicode{x2669}.} = \mathrel{\unicode{x2669}}$)

Allegretto con moto

In the light of that star Lie the a-ges im-pearled, And that

song from a-far Has swept o-ver the world; Ev-'ry heart is a-flame While the Beau-ti-ful sing, In the homes of the na-tions, That Je-sus is King. We re-joice in the light _____ And we ech - o the song _____ That comes down thro' the night _____ From the heav'n - ly throng. Aye, __ we shout _____ to the love - ly __ E - van - gel they bring, And __ we greet in His

f < ff grandioso

cra - dle our Sav - iour and King, And we

accel. e cresc. al fine

greet in His cra - dle our

opt. rit.

Sav - iour, our Sav - iour and

colla voce

lento

King!

ff *lento e pesante*

The Virgin at the Manger
(La Vierge à la Crêche)

Alphonse Daudet

A. Périlhou

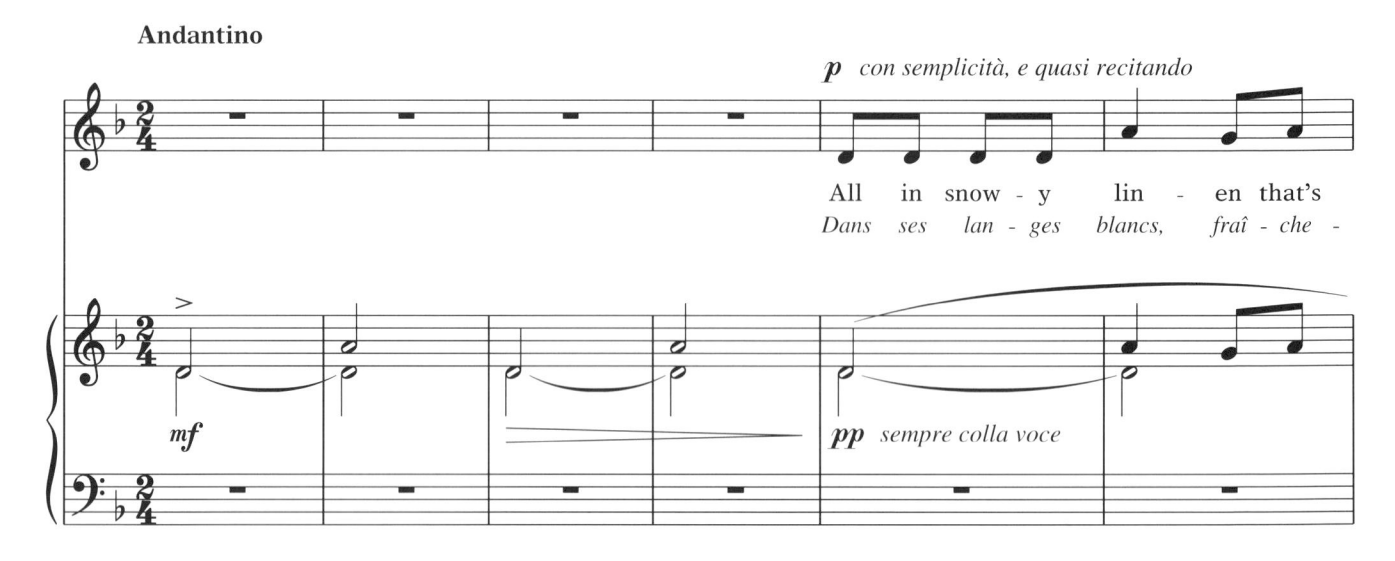

Andantino

p con semplicità, e quasi recitando

All in snow-y lin-en that's new-ly sewn, Mar-y hath en-cra-dled the Child, her own,
Dans ses langes blancs, fraîche-ment cou-sus, La Vierge berçait son enfant Jésus.

Je-sus lies lisp-ing like nes-tled star-lings, Moth-er-ly she ber-
Lui gazouillait comme un nid de mésanges. Elle le ber-

rocks him with rapture deep, Singing just as we sing to
çait et chan-tait tout bas Ce que nous chan-tons à nos

sleep-y dar-lings But her lit-tle Child will not go to sleep.
pe-tits an-ges— Màis l'en-fant Jé-sus ne s'en-dor-mait pas.

Allegro moderato

Charmed by the mu-sic that croons a-
É-ton-né, ra-vi, de ce qu'il en-

long, Laugh-ing, as he lies there, he joins her song,
tend, Il rit dans sa crèche, et s'en va chan-tant,

Feel-ing in his spir-it the me-lo-dy in-spir-ing, Both his hands up-lift-ed, the mea-sures keep; But the moth-er, watch-ing with love un-tir-ing, Sighs be-cause her Child will not go to sleep.

Comme un saint lé-vite et comme un cho-ris-te Il bat la me-sure a-vec ses deux bras. Et la sain-te Vierge est tris-te, bien tris-te, De voir son Jé-sus qui ne s'en-dort pas.

Andante

Mar-y, wan and sad, and with tear-ful smile,

Et Ma-rie a-lors, le re-gard voi-lé,

Bends a-bove the Child where he wakes the while. "Moth-er has to cry, if you
Pen-che sur son fils un front dé-so-lé: "Vous ne dor-mez pas, vo-tre

will not shut your eyes, now, Pre-cious lit-tle man, you make moth-er
mè - re ___ pleu - re, Vo-tre mè-re pleure, o mon bel a-

weep." And lo! as her tears o-ver-flow, in this hour
mi." Des lar-mes cou-laient de ses yeux; sur l'heu-

now, Gen-tle Ba-by Je-sus is fast a-sleep.
re, Le pe-tit Jé-sus s'é-tait en-dor-mi.

The Virgin's Slumber Song
(Mariä Wiegenlied)

Martin Boelitz

Max Reger

Allegretto

A - mid the ros - es Mar - y sits and rocks her Je - sus child, While a - mid the tree - tops sighs the breeze so warm and mild.

Ma - ri - a sitzt am Ro - sen - hag und wiegt ihr Je - sus - kind, durch die Blät - ter lei - se weht der war - me Som - mer - wind.

Copyright © 2001 by HAL LEONARD CORPORATION
International Copyright Secured   All Rights Reserved

And soft and sweet - ly sings a bird upon the bough;
Zu ih - ren Fü - ssen singt ein bun - tes Vö - ge - lein:

Ah, ba - by, dear one,
Schlaf', Kind - lein, sü - sse,

slum - ber now!
schlaf' nun ein!

Hap - py is Thy laugh - ter, ho - ly is Thy
Hold ist dein Lä - cheln, hol - der dei - nes

si - lent rest, Lay Thy head in slum - ber, fond - ly on Thy
Schlum - mers Lust, leg dein mü - des Köpf - chen fest an dei - ner

Moth - er's breast! Ah, ba - by,
Mut - ter Brust! Schlaf', Kind - lein,

dear _____ one, slum -
sü _____ sse, schlaf' _____

- ber now!
nun ein!

The Christmas Song
(Chestnuts Roasting on an Open Fire)

Music and Lyric by Mel Torme and Robert Wells

Sentimentally

Chest- nuts roast- ing on an o- pen fire, Jack Frost nip- ping at your nose, yule- tide car- ols being sung by a choir and folks dressed up like Es- ki- mos. Ev- 'ry- body

© 1946 (Renewed) EDWIN H. MORRIS & COMPANY, A Division of MPL Communications, Inc.
All Rights Reserved

knows a tur-key and some mis-tle-toe help to make the sea-son bright. Ti-ny tots with their eyes all a-glow will find it hard to sleep to-night. They know that San-ta's on his way; he's load-ed lots of toys and good-ies on his sleigh, and ev-'ry mother's child is gonna spy to see if reindeer really know how to fly. And so I'm offering this simple phrase to kids from one to ninety-two. Although it's been said many times, many ways, "Merry Christmas to you." you."

Voices of the Sky
from *The Story of Christmas*

H. Alexander Matthews

Andante con espressione

O love-ly voic-es of the sky, That hymn'd the Sav-iour's birth! Are ye not sing-ing, sing-ing still on high, are ye not sing-ing,

Copyright © 2001 by HAL LEONARD CORPORATION
International Copyright Secured

sing-ing still on high, are ye not sing - ing, sing-ing still on high,

Ye that sang, "Peace on earth?" To us yet speak, yet speak ___ the strains, Where-with, in days gone by, Ye bless'd the Syr - ian swains, O voic - es of the sky, Ye bless'd the Syr - ian swains, ___ O voic - es of the sky! O love - ly voic - es, love - ly voic - es of the sky, That hymn'd ___ the Sav - iour's

dim. e rit. *a tempo*

opt.

slentando

birth!

rit. *mp* *a tempo*

O clear and shin-ing

p sotto voce

light! whose beams That hour heav'n's glo-ry___ shed A-

cresc.

round the palms and o'er the streams, And on the shep - herd's

head; Be near, through life and death, As in that ho- liest night Of Hope, and Joy, of Joy, and Faith, O clear and shin- ing light! O lovely voices of the sky, That hymn'd the Saviour's birth? Be near in life, in death, As in that holiest night.

What Songs Were Sung

By John Jacob Niles

Tenderly ♩ = c. 66 *(in a story-telling manner)*

We can-not tell, we do not know What stars shone down so long a-go, When Mar-y birthed her own sweet Son And peace and love be-

Copyright © 1965 (Renewed) by G. Schirmer, Inc. (ASCAP), New York, NY
International Copyright Secured   All Rights Reserved
Reprinted by Permission

came as one. The Son of God, as scrip-tures said, Was Vir-gin born in a ti-ny shed, Where sim-ple shep-herds stood hard by While heav'n-ly sound filled up the sky. Now let us stand, uncov - ered all, Be - fore this crèche in ___ low - ly stall, Where kings and an - gels dig - ni - fy God's __ gift, His Son, in hu - mil - i - ty. We do not know, we can - not tell What songs were sung, what __ star - light fell, Or

why the ho-ly mys-ter-y stands For so man-y years in so man-y lands. We can-not tell, we do not know What stars shone down so long a-go, When Mar-y birthed her own sweet Son And peace and love be-came as one.

White Christmas
from the Motion Picture Irving Berlin's HOLIDAY INN

Words and Music by Irving Berlin

The sun is shin-ing, the grass is green, the or-ange and palm trees sway. There's nev-er been such a day in Bev-er-ly Hills, L. A.

© Copyright 1940, 1942 by Irving Berlin
Copyright Renewed
International Copyright Secured   All Rights Reserved

But it's December the twenty-fourth, and I am longing to be up north.

I'm dreaming of a white Christmas, just like the

ones I used to know, where the tree-tops glisten and children listen to hear sleigh bells in the snow. I'm dreaming of a white Christmas with ev-'ry Christ-mas card I write: "May your days be mer-ry and bright, and may all your Christ-mas-es be white." white."

Do You Hear What I Hear

Words and Music by Noel Regney and Gloria Shayne

Gently

Said the night-wind to the lit-tle lamb,
lit-tle lamb to the shep-herd boy,
shep-herd boy to the might-y king,

Do you see what I see? ___ 'Way up in the sky, lit-tle lamb,
Do you hear what I hear? ___ Ring-ing thru the sky, shep-herd boy,
Do you know what I know? ___ In your pal-ace warm, might-y king,

Do you see what I see? ___ A star, a star,
Do you hear what I hear? ___ A song, a song,
Do you know what I know? ___ A Child, a Child

Copyright © 1962 by Regent Music Corporation (BMI)
Copyright Renewed by Jewel Music Publishing Co., Inc. (ASCAP)
International Copyright Secured All Rights Reserved
Used by Permission

Dancing in the night, with a tail as big as a kite, With a tail as big as a kite.
High a-bove the tree, with a voice as big as the sea, With a voice as big as the sea.
shiv-ers in the cold; Let us bring Him sil-ver and gold, Let us bring Him sil-ver and gold.

1,2 Said the

3 Said the king to the peo-ple ev-'ry-where, Lis-ten to what I say! Pray for peace, peo-ple ev-'ry-where, Lis-ten to what I say! The Child; The Child, sleep-ing in the night; He will bring us good-ness and light, He will bring us good-ness and light.